I0168104

Strange Sightings and Mysterious Creatures in the New Forest and Beyond

by
Alison Crocker

Grosvenor House
Publishing Limited

All rights reserved
Copyright © Alison Crocker, 2020

The right of Alison Crocker to be identified as the author of this
work has been asserted in accordance with Section 78
of the Copyright, Designs and Patents Act 1988

The book cover is copyright to Alison Crocker

This book is published by
Grosvenor House Publishing Ltd
Link House
140 The Broadway, Tolworth, Surrey, KT6 7HT.
www.grosvenorhousepublishing.co.uk

This book is sold subject to the conditions that it shall not, by way of
trade or otherwise, be lent, resold, hired out or otherwise circulated
without the author's or publisher's prior consent in any form of binding or
cover other than that in which it is published and
without a similar condition including this condition being imposed
on the subsequent purchaser.

This book is a work of fiction. Any resemblance to
people or events, past or present, is purely coincidental.

A CIP record for this book
is available from the British Library

ISBN 978-1-83975-068-7

Also available in eBook format
ISBN 978-1-83975-069-4

ACKNOWLEDGEMENTS

This book is dedicated to all the mystery seekers across the globe. Those who tirelessly research, write and explore locations. I also want to thank my sons Jason and Tom for putting up with my ramblings about the paranormal for years and years.

I also want to thank Jessica from Coleman Editing for helping me turn my stories and witness accounts into a book.

Finally, a big thank you to my You Tube subscribers for sending me their stories, photos and accounts. Without you, this book would not have been possible.

INTRODUCTION

The New Forest is a wonderful, magical place that is home to many strange sightings and mysterious creatures – you just have to know where to look.

I have lived mostly in the New Forest, and in that time I've had many personal experiences and sightings that defy logical explanation. These incidents, along with my lifetime fascination with mysteries and the unexplained, are why I decided to write this book.

A couple of years ago I decided to start logging these experiences on a website, on which I asked others to share their own stories. Consequently, people started sending me their accounts by email, and I started adding the locations of these encounters to a map on the site, along with the details. What interests me most is the similarity of the accounts given by so many people, completely unknown to each other, happening at the exact same locations time and time again. What other explanation is there other than that the New Forest is full of intriguing, mysterious secrets?

I wanted to write this book to share these secrets with you.

Perhaps you've had your own experiences in the area, strange occurrences you can't explain or that keep you up at night?

If so, please read on – and see if any of these stories ring any bells.

A Brief History of this
Magical Place

Located in Southern England and consisting of 218 square miles, the New Forest is the smallest national park in the country, though there is nothing small about its beauty and rich cultural heritage. This stunning area is absolutely filled with interesting history – some of it mysterious and intriguing, and some of it downright spooky.

There are few areas of England where – throughout the decades and centuries – the landscape has remained relatively unchanged, but the New Forest is definitely one of them. In fact, 1000 years ago William the Conqueror called it 'his new hunting forest', and the land today isn't much different to how it would have been back then. This is due, in part, to the protective structure William established in order to manage the woodlands and wild heathlands, a structure that is still very much in place today.

Later came the Tudor and Elizabethan influences, when Britain's most famous monarch, Henry VIII, commissioned both Hurst Castle and Calshot Castle to be built, as well as owning a monastery at Beaulieu.

As well as its royal connections, the New Forest also played an important part in both world wars. For instance, when Breamore House near Fordingbridge was taken over by the military it was visited by General Patton, the village of Brockenhurst saw wounded World War I soldiers treated for their injuries in makeshift hospitals, and Generals Eisenhower and Montgomery met at Balmer Lawn in Brockenhurst as they plotted the famous D-day invasion. Ashley Walk near

Fordingbridge was used to test the 'bouncing bomb', and there were 12 airfields in total across the whole area, remnants of which can still be seen today.

I have a personal interest in World War II because I believe I have a past life memory of this time. Due to this, I have visited some of the 12 airfields of the New Forest (sadly, some of them can't be visited due to their location), and have obtained some interesting material there.

Over the centuries this area has been no stranger to unusual sightings, and no wonder – the forest is magical, steeped in a 1000 year-long mystical history that encompasses everything from ghosts and hauntings to weird and wonderful creature sightings.

Beginning

My interest in the paranormal began around 1986 when, fresh from school, I started at my boring office job. My colleagues and I would chat in between typing letters and doing accounts, and one day – probably to alleviate our mutual boredom – we got onto the subject of dreams. In turn, each of us would recall the previous night's dreams, how we felt about them, and what we thought they meant. I then bought a dream interpretation book from my local bookshop and we began loosely deciphering each dream meaning. My curiosity was aroused when some of the dreams seemed to symbolise actual events and even appeared to offer solutions to problems.

An example of this would be my colleague dreaming about cats. In her dream, there were cats everywhere in the street where she lived. They sat on car roofs, pavements, fences, driveways, and so on. Cats are an ancient symbol of increasing psychic power and a strongly awakening sixth sense. Looking back, this was the start of her psychic journey, because two years later she went to work as a secretary for a workshop facilitator for psychic studies.

When we are on the right path people just 'pop up', seeming to appear just at the right time to help us along. The word journey is so overused these days; I prefer to call it spiritual path.

It was a couple of years after the boring office job that I came across an ad in a local paper for people of a like mind to join a spiritual development group, led by a medium. I was nervous as I attended the first class, but I needn't have been as everyone was very friendly. It was at one of these weekly sessions that I had my first encounter with Spirit.

During previous sessions, whilst being guided through a group meditation, I had 'felt' something behind me – that feeling you get when someone is standing really close behind you. I remember jolting during the meditation, disrupting everyone's peaceful thoughts, as I could feel the energy of a tongue in my mouth, only it wasn't mine. I opened my eyes to find that I felt 6 feet tall (I'm 5ft 2), and that I was looking down at everyone, staring. It felt so real and yet so disconnected at the same time. I admit to being very scared. Clearly, an energy had taken me over and I was now someone else.

My memory of what happened next is vague. I think I might have fainted as when I came around I was lying on the floor with everyone standing around me, a dozen concerned faces peering down at me.

My first experience of what is known as Trance Mediumship took me weeks to get over. The trained medium attending the group said I'd been taken over by a very powerful entity and that I hadn't been able to take it. Looking back, I was so young – around 18 at the time – that I didn't really know what to make of it all.

Even so, I carried on attending the group, gaining more experience through exercises like table tipping, séances, dowsing, and practising clairvoyance. I had started reading Tarot cards by now too, and was giving readings part time whilst working full time. Developing psychically takes discipline and commitment and I'm glad I continued, even though at times it was difficult.

Whilst I've always been aware of Spirit, my abilities seemed to go up a notch when strange events appeared to accelerate my spiritual awareness. I eventually went from sensing spirits to seeing them, my turning point coming in 2004. At the time I was living in West Sussex with my husband, commuting regularly between Midhurst and Chichester. The area is beautiful, with green rolling hills on both sides of the road, and we were fortunate enough to have a car each. He worked locally and I was a full-time mother to two toddlers.

One day around teatime, after a walk around the shops at Chichester, I was travelling back with my children along the A286 – the busy road that connects Midhurst to Chichester – when, as the car took a sweeping bend, I noticed a lady running across the road in front of me, headed towards a public house about 400 yards away. What was strange about this was that she was wearing a long cloak with the hood over her head – I remember thinking what strange attire to wear in this day and age! I couldn't see all of her face, only the profile, but she seemed to be around 20-30 years old. She appeared in front of me for about two seconds and then she vanished. I wasn't scared, just mystified, and when I arrived home I told my husband what I'd seen and then thought no more of it.

A few days later, I was travelling along the same stretch of road at around 9 pm when, upon reaching the spot where I'd seen the mysterious cloaked woman, the headlights on my car went out for a few seconds before coming back on again. This was frightening because the A286 is unlit for long stretches, and there were no cars either behind or in front of me. I managed to get home without further incident and told my husband, who suggested that the next day we should swap cars to see if the same thing happened to him. Relieved, I agreed.

The next day, alone once again, I made my way along the A286 at dusk in my husband's car, and as soon as I got to that spot, the headlights went out again. I was scared, but I vowed to solve this mystery.

Upon arriving home, my husband leapt out of his chair as I came through the front door, saying he had something to tell me. He went on to explain that he'd mentioned what had been going on with the headlights to a colleague at work. This colleague was a local man and knew a lot of history, and he explained to my husband that during the 1800s a woman had been killed at that very spot by a horse and cart whilst crossing the road, headed for the public house.

At least now I had an explanation, if a very sad one.

I continued to read Tarot cards for people, offering spiritual healing in my home and sometimes travelling to see poorly people. Sadly, my husband and I divorced not long after the headlight incident, and I moved back to Hampshire. There, in 2010, I qualified as a Spiritual Healer with the National Federation of Spiritual Healers, having begun my training in 2004 as a single parent. There was something about the training that seemed to open the door for me; it's as if it all started to make sense, with the recent trauma of my separation from my husband, as well as my eldest son's recent diagnosis of Autism at the age of three, seeming to be helped by my training. I felt as if I was finally on my spiritual path and that I was meant to be there.

Don't get me wrong, there were times when I could have just sat and cried into my cornflakes every morning as I felt so alone and disappointed, having never thought I'd end up as single parent. No one ever does. I believe we all set out with the best intentions and then suffer when things don't pan out in the way we'd imagined. It's a form of shock.

The flat I moved into in Southampton was horrible, but as I was desperate, I took on the tenancy anyway. Situated in a block of 12, I was on the second floor, and the noise from the main road close by meant that on warm nights I had to sleep with the window closed as the noise from the traffic was deafening, even at night. There was usually a two-hour respite between the hours of 2 and 4 am, but then it would start again. As well as this, the guy upstairs from me kept snakes, one of which escaped and went missing for several weeks, so for safety I had to keep the windows closed. I had horrible visions of this 6ft thing sliding down the wall and into my room. I always felt unsafe living there, and really vulnerable; I'm from quite a rural part of Hampshire originally, and city life is very different.

One morning, after yet another restless sleep, I walked into my kitchen to see a 7-foot-tall shimmering being standing there, looking out of the window, his arms crossed in a defensive pose.

At first, I wasn't sure what I was seeing. He didn't look at me but instead gave off an aura of peace, calm, and protection. I had seen images of Archangel Michael on some cards that I sometimes used, and after watching for a few moments, I knew it was him.

I stood staring at the figure for what felt like ages, then I felt compelled to leave the kitchen and come back in again, as if to make sure that what I was seeing was actually there. I did, and he was. I was wide awake and definitely not hallucinating. Strangely, I felt no need to talk to 'him'; it's as if his presence was enough.

I just *knew* from this encounter that everything was going to be alright. I had the feeling of receiving an inner hug, as if I'd been lifted up on a carpet of white wings, and surrounded by a feeling of total protection and peace.

Not long after this, I moved back to my hometown.

High Strangeness

To many people, the idea of a British Bigfoot seems laughable, and personally, I've noticed that there are two camps of belief. The first camp are in absolutely no doubt that there is a 7ft hairy bipedal meandering around the wilderness of our UK forests, whereas the second think it not even possible due to the small size of the British Isles. My own thoughts are not as cut and dried as some.

And it isn't just Bigfoot that's captured people's imaginations. I have a number of other unusual sightings on my books, some from everyday folk who were simply going about their business, walking their dog, when all of a sudden, they encountered something rather strange. Many people say that Bigfoot only really exists in the States, probably because the wilderness over there really *is* the wilderness; Yosemite National Park in California, for instance, covers approximately 750,000 acres, its dense forests going on for miles and miles. Many parts of these forests have never seen humans, and those that do may only see them for a short period, whilst they're logging or camping or following a trail on foot. There are far more places, therefore, for Bigfoot (and any number of other mysterious creatures) to hide.

If that's the case, what's going on in the UK? And where exactly are they hiding in the much smaller British Isles?

The New Forest could have the answer.

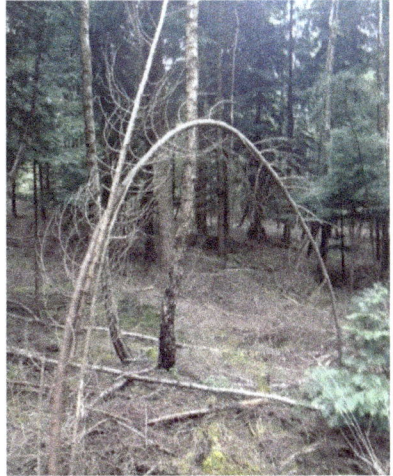

New Forest tree structures © Suzanne Singleton

The Silence

I have certainly felt unusual presences whilst being out in the forest, filming for my YouTube videos alone, but I always try to remain open-minded. These incidents always begin the same way: with what is known as 'the silence'. During the silence all birdsong stops as an eerie atmosphere descends, much like a dark cloud. These strange occurrences are accompanied by a deep, lingering sense of dread, as well as the feeling that one should leave the area immediately. The eeriness is tangible. It is like stepping into another dimension.

Although the surroundings remain the same, the atmosphere changes completely; while the forest stays the same, our perception of it seems to change, our senses becoming significantly heightened. What creates this atmospheric change is unknown, though it isn't something that comes from within me or any other individuals who've experienced something strange; something occurring outside of us makes these changes.

Could it be that Bigfoot makes these alterations, possibly to scare us, to make us retreat back from whence we came? Could it be that whoever instigates these changes doesn't want humans around because of a general lack of trust? I feel this is quite justifiable. After all, it is man who cuts down trees and destroys the habitats of wild animals so he can build more homes… it is man who, in the form of hunters, kill innocent creatures for pleasure. Why wouldn't they have a safety mechanism, a security procedure to protect them from those who might hurt them?

Portals

I believe in portals. These are certain places around the world where lots of paranormal events have been witnessed, and where the likelihood of experiencing something weird is significantly higher. I would describe a portal as being a veil between this world and the next, where the atmosphere is 'thinner' than other places and where tears in the fabric of time can also occur. When these 'tears' occur, we might experience a time slip or a warping of time. I am fortunate to have experienced this for myself.

Over the years I've received many accounts of strange things happening to ordinary folk whilst they've been out enjoying their leisure time in the New Forest. For instance, on more than one occasion I've received photos of trees with slim trunks standing in excess of 15 feet tall, snapped off at a height of at least eight feet. A clean break. What breaks a tree in half this far up? As well as these I've also received photos of perfectly formed arches, where a long branch has been arched with one end 'pinned' by something else.

Stranger still, in a comment from someone who watched my YouTube channel, I've received a report of a 'tree spirit' joining a couple when they were out for a stroll. This man was out walking with a friend in some woods just north of Southampton when they saw a fairy with a smiling face, appearing directly in front of them for just a moment before vanishing again.

As well as this tree spirit, I've heard of several other appearances from fairies and nature spirits, all catching unsuspecting nature lovers off guard.

Basically, a tree spirit or tree deity is any kind of nature deity that is related to a tree. Such deities – which are often connected to ancient fertility and tree worship lore – are present in many cultures, and are usually represented as a young woman. Some people call these fairies or sprites, while others use the term nymph, ghost, or goddess.

Trees of all kinds are significant in many of the world's mythologies and religions, and have been given sacred meanings throughout the ages as humans have observed their growth, life, and death cycle. Consequently, trees have long been powerful symbols of growth and rebirth.

Tree lore is the study of this cycle, as well as the meanings of individual species of trees. For instance, Oak represents stability and strength, and to the Celts, the Yew tree means death and regeneration.

A regular dog walker has told me that her dog behaves strangely in certain parts of the forest, either barking furiously at thin air or cowering, as if in the presence of a supernatural being – or, at the very least, as if in the presence of something that instils a deep fear into the animal. The same witness showed me an image she had taken on her mobile phone of what looks like a pair of creature's eyes peering out of the dense bushes. I was taken aback by this photo, as the eyes can be seen clearly.

One night, several tourists were camping in a popular part of the forest, and having had an uneventful night's sleep, they awoke to hear disturbing growling noises, not far from their tents. Another time, a cyclist emailed me after seeing a huge 7ft hairy man in the woods just off the cycle track. This cyclist comes to the New Forest, alone, to go on cycling holidays, and this particular time he was cycling through a stretch of woodland along the former single-track railway (now a cycle path). It was here where he became aware of seeing something large – a brown humanoid shape – flitting between the trees. As the witness was partially disabled and with an arthritic condition, he couldn't reach for his mobile phone in time to take a picture.

Surprisingly, the cyclist reports that he didn't feel scared – just curious.

Rocks have been thrown by unseen forces, while bangs and thuds have been heard and felt vibrating through the forest floor, seemingly without explanation.

A dog walker described finding a feather tied to a tree at the Anderwood BBQ centre, where visitors can hire barbecue hearths or have a picnic. This seems to be an active area as I've had quite a few reports from the centre. Feathers are typically part of Native American symbology and are given as gifts as a sign of honour, power, respect, and dignity. I'm not for one minute suggesting that Bigfoot ties these feathers to bushes and trees as a way of communicating; I think it's more plausible that this is the work of human beings wishing to make contact with the creatures in the forest, but I cannot be certain.

Burley, New Forest – it gets even stranger!

In the summer of 2018, a trip to some woods in this ancient village resulted in me capturing some startling evidence on video. I went alone, armed with my video camera, to make a video about the Oldfield Filter and how it produces captivating pictures by capturing invisible light.

Whilst filming I became aware that I wasn't alone, even though there was no one around apart from a few people some 800 metres away in a car park, enjoying a picnic.

It was an incredibly hot day, there was no breeze, and as it was muggy and unbearable to walk around, I found a relatively comfortable spot on a pathway while I made my video. I was aware of some footsteps approaching me and I expected to see someone come into view as they got closer, but no one arrived and the footsteps seemed to walk past me a few metres away. I was grateful I had caught the audio on camera. Then, suddenly, as my camcorder was pointing straight ahead at a small bush, I was stunned to see unseen hands – or some other kind of invisible force – move the bush to one side as they walked past. I was lucky to have caught this on video. Who or what had moved the bush?

I sat there for a few minutes trying to find a rational explanation for what I'd just seen. There was no breeze, no wind, and nothing else to cause the bush to move in that way. To this day, my only explanation is that I caught a spirit being as he or she passed through the area. Even before the bush had moved, I *knew* something was there because I could hear it and sense it.

What the heck is that? – a witness account, Ashley, New Milton

I was walking to work at about 4.30 am way back, I'd say, in about 2015. It was pouring with rain and as I approached Ashley crossroads next to the shops, I saw a figure emerge from a bush a little further down the road, opposite the Ashley pub (which is now the Nisa shop). It kind of reminded me of how the old pink panther dressed, the big hat and overcoat. It was weird, not because of how it looked but because of how it moved: it kind of jumped like a kangaroo, hopping along the road and clearing a long distance very quickly. It had a very long nose like a bird's beak and it held a pose in a weird way. It then disappeared behind the rugby club. It was pitch black that night but I got a good look at it because the road was brightly lit by street lamps. It struck me as odd because in five years I'd not seen anybody out at that time of the morning, and the issue of it performing odd super-human-like movements was all just so weird.

Witness drawing of sighting.

Haunted Road
Ringwood, Hampshire

I received this account recently from someone who gave me his full name, but I'll change it to James.

James, a cyclist, had an unnerving experience on a forest road.

The first time I personally heard about this spooky road was back in 1993. Someone who knew of my interest in ghosts approached me in a pub one night and told me the story of two friends who lived in nearby Ringwood, who were using this road to travel to Cadnam. There are no cat's eyes, no road markings, and no streetlights nearby, and only a few houses and two pubs along the route. The surrounding area is open heathlands as it's close to former WWII airfield, Stoney Cross, and there are a few wooded areas heading back towards the Red Shoot Inn and the High Corner Inn. Within the last year or so, the council have put in passing places because it is so narrow (really only wide enough for one car); if you're unlucky enough to meet someone travelling in the opposite direction, things can get a bit tricky.

The pair claim they were chased at high speed by a large black limousine, which they described as a hearse. It was a cold, wet, and windy autumnal night, and as they drove they found themselves being tailgated by this menacing black vehicle that travelled just inches from their rear bumper. Then it simply disappeared, vanishing into thin air only to reappear in front of them a mile or so later.

By now they were both feeling terrified, and anxious to get to their destination. It was then that their car lost all its power.

So, standing on the side of the lonely road in total darkness, they looked under the bonnet – a little torch their only source of light – mystified at the car's sudden and alarming problem. Then the headlights of a vehicle pulled in behind them and they both sighed with relief, thinking it was someone coming to help... but no one got out of the car. The car raced off and as it sped by, they realised it was the black limo again!

As soon as the mystery vehicle had driven off, their car engine started, the headlights shone again, and the wipers started working. Both made it to Cadnam, but they've vowed never to travel that route again at night.

Speaking of the same location, James gave me the following witness account:

The year was 2012, and James was out cycling around this picturesque road of the New Forest. He says he first saw a young boy with a bicycle who was soaked through to the skin just past the High Corner Inn. The boy looked like he had just stepped out of the '70s, with blond hair, a blue T-shirt with red piping, and flares. James describes his bike as being a girl's Raleigh.

James felt uneasy about this sighting, so he just kept pedalling.

He later saw the same boy, still soaked to the skin, by Janesmoor Pond, a few miles past the High Corner. There's no way he could have passed him.

I love receiving stories like this. Two accounts, 19 years apart, involving the same seemingly impossible manoeuvre, where people and vehicles appear in front of you and behind you at random, with no possible means of explanation.

Isle of Wight – Hampshire

Ley lines are lines of invisible energy that run all over the world, connecting ancient sites or monuments; their alignments are of prehistoric and religious significance, and where they cross is often the location of a church or a special magical place. There are debates, however, about whether these actually exist, as they are really only detectable using a pendulum or dowsing rods, though sometimes people can feel these ley lines – at such places as Glastonbury and Avebury, for instance – due to their sheer power.

One of the main ley lines in Britain is the Belinus Line, which travels downwards through the whole of the UK and which was named by a monk called Geoffrey of Monmouth back around 1100 AD. Belinus, he wrote, was a descendant of Trojan Brutus (or 'Brutus of Troy'), the mythical founder of Britain who had ruled over the kingdom of Cornwall. He ordered this straight road to be built, going through many cities and places of sanctuary, so people would have somewhere to go where they could feel safe.

The ley lines on the Isle of Wight seem particularly energised, although not quite in the same way as the ones at Stonehenge, Avebury, or Glastonbury.

I've always described this island as an island of two halves, with Newport being roughly in the centre. To the north of Newport there's Cowes, Yarmouth, and views across the Solent to the South Coast mainland. The energies in the north feel fresh and vibrant. However, the areas to the south of Newport have a totally different feel to them. There's a darkness to these places, and when you're in them it's like you're surrounded by a heavy black cloud and a deep sense of foreboding.

A few years ago, I decided to holiday there, and during my trip I went to Ventnor Botanic Garden, which was formally a hospital. Opening in 1869, the hospital closed in 1964 due to the introduction of drug treatments for tuberculosis. The building was demolished in 1969 with the botanical gardens opening the next year, in 1970.

When I visited the gardens, I conversed with the spirit of a man who had been a patient there in the 1940s. When I saw him he was sitting by a garden ornament as he smoked a cigarette, and so clear was this energy that I can even describe what he was wearing: a white shirt and brown trousers. He appeared to be aged around 40, with red hair and a pale complexion.

He told me he'd been sent to the hospital to recover from tuberculosis but that he'd never got better and had died. He also told me that he knew he would never leave the hospital, but that it didn't matter – he was quite content to stay there. Not all spirit beings want to leave the places they find themselves in, and I believe that if they want to stay, they should. This man had a lively, charming, pleasant personality and seemed happy to chat to me.

Other sections of the gardens weren't as pleasant; lower down towards the sea, I had the feeling of not being able to breathe, and given that the place used to be a hospital for patients suffering from chest diseases, this feeling wasn't surprising.

Another place I visited on the Isle of Wight was Blackgang Chine, which is the creepiest theme park I've ever been to. I was part of an all-night paranormal investigation there in 2008.

Having opened in 1836, Blackgang Chine is Britain's oldest theme park, and over the years so much tragedy has occurred here that it's really left its mark; the atmosphere is both oppressive and ominous. In 1836 the cargo ship the Clarendon was shipwrecked at the foot of Blackgang Chine, with all onboard being lost.

During the investigation I attended, another ghost hunter caught a red orb on camera – completely red. In my experience, this is a signal that all is not well in this location, as red orbs can indicate unpleasant energies and beings.

Strange Cloaked Entity

Last year, whilst stargazing in my back garden – something I do regularly as we don't have much light pollution here – something happened. The sky was completely black, apart from the very distant orange glow coming from the streetlights in Bournemouth on the south coast, and after a few minutes, I suddenly became frozen with fear – utterly and completely. I remember holding my breath and gasping. Within a couple of seconds of this, I saw what I can only describe as a black cloaked entity land on my neighbours' shed roof. I saw no facial features or even a humanoid outline, just something cloaked. The black was blacker than black. It was big too – my guess would be 8-9 feet tall, like an enormous flying black sheet –and it blocked out a few of the stars in the distance. Within a few seconds, the entity disappeared and the feeling of terror left me as quickly as it had come. However, I was so spooked about this event that I went inside and didn't go back outside again that night.

This wasn't the first time something like this had happened.

I've also seen something peering over the edge of my shed roof, literally just for one second before it's gone again. These occurrences, however, don't carry with them the same feeling of terror. Again, it's a black formless entity but much smaller than the large entity I saw on my neighbours' roof.

Researching this topic on the internet threw up a few stories similar to mine, although one person in particular felt the cloaked figure was haunting them, having had four encounters in his life so far. His description was that of a skeleton wearing a cloak – which also ties into a sleep paralysis experience – plus a rancid, rotting smell.

My second true story was told to me by my very level-headed 19-year-old son, who's very down to earth and not generally given to flights of fancy and imagined events. He has an interest in the paranormal but it doesn't consume him.

One-night last autumn, my son awoke suddenly at around 1 am. He doesn't know what woke him, he was just suddenly wide awake. He notes that he was facing his bedroom window, and that the drapes at the window were closed (they're not blackout drapes because there's no light out the back as the two streetlights we have nearby are too far away to make any difference). Within ten seconds or so he witnessed a huge white flash similar to that of a huge flashlight beam, lighting up the window for a second and then turning off again. He doesn't remember anything else. He told me he wasn't scared – just curious – and that he soon drifted off back to sleep. We aren't overlooked, and there are no roads at the back, so it couldn't have been headlights. Neither was it lightning, because the flashes were directly outside of the window.

We tried to recreate what he saw, with me going out and flashing a torch at the window for a second and then turning if off. He said it had been similar to that only much, much brighter.

It's not happened since. Thankfully.

Flash of Light – Alderbury, Wiltshire

Twenty years ago, my then husband and I were taking a shortcut home through a field (he worked this land and so knew it well), as our house was located at the bottom. It was around February and approximately 8 pm, so still dark, and we didn't have a torch. We lived in a rural village that had several streetlights dotted about, but there were none anywhere near the field or our home.

As we climbed the five-bar gate and started to make our way across the field towards the house, I was a little spooked, I have to say. Suddenly, there was a flash that lit up the whole field as clear as day. It was just for a second, but it was so bright we could see everything momentarily: the grass, the trees, the bushes, everything. My husband asked what it was, and I said I had no idea. I didn't have a clue. It seemed to come from above us – but not from the sky – and it only appeared to light up our immediate surroundings. It was as if the light had come from 100 metres up, and besides, it was far too bright to have been car headlights. It was as if the sun had shone directly down on us, just for a second.

After that we sped up; I couldn't wait to reach the safety of my front door.

World War II – A Flashback

My interest in WWII began in 2008, when I had an experience whilst training to be a Past Life Regression Therapist. At this point I was literally haunted by a dream I'd started having a few years prior to this, and I just had to know why this dream was never very far from my thoughts. It was one of the dreams where when you wake, you feel as if it had actually happened. You awake tired and on edge, and I certainly felt that way every time I woke up from this dream. Many people experience dreams like this.

In my dream, I was a young German man aged 19. I was a reluctant soldier; I didn't want to fight and had never killed anyone. I was walking through a muddy field that had no coverage. It was completely bare, with not even one tree or hedgerow, and it was like this as far as the eye could see. I had the impression I was in Northern France because a house I could see in the distance had shutters, which reminded me of a French Chateau. I also knew I'd been with a group of people, although they had since wandered away from me. I feel these people were also soldiers, as we felt part of a unit, but even so I had distanced myself from them – why I don't know.

I slowly edged forward. I was holding my rifle, my finger frozen to the trigger, and I felt exhausted and tired. The mud clinging to my boots was cold and heavy. I could no longer feel my feet as I edged forward, and I was consumed by the most terrifying feeling. I was so scared.

I know that in my dream I was being watched, but I couldn't see by whom. Slowly, I looked down at my hands. They had lost their normal fleshy appearance and colour and were now a worrying purply blue shade. They were freezing.

Suddenly, I saw movement in the corner of my eye. A figure in the distance had stood up from a trench I hadn't been aware of. I saw him take aim, and literally a second later... BANG!

I had been shot in my left side.

I fell forward, landing face down in the thick, freezing mud. I remember how it felt as my life force drained away. As my vision slowly weakened and my breathing became laboured, the pain that had sliced through me started to lessen. Quick, fleeting thoughts of what felt like a pointless life came rushing into my mind, racing thoughts about everything I wouldn't get to experience and everything I wished I'd done filling my entire being.

Then, suddenly, nothing. A void of blackness, blacker than black.

I still get flashbacks of this dream from time to time, usually triggered by something I see or hear, such as a TV programme or a piece of music from World War Two.

I've never forgotten this dream, and it's still so sharp in my mind – even to this day. I can go back to it at any moment, and all the details are always still there, vivid and as clear as day.

I believe we experience things like this at the right time for us – and for me, it was the right time for me to experience this sad yet intriguing dream.

RAF Ibsley – Ringwood, Hampshire

It was a warm spring day at the former WWII site, which is now a glorious nature reserve with many lakes. The old concrete slabs of the runway are still visible, revealing intriguing glimpses into the past. It's hard to really get an impression of how it would have looked back at the time of the war, although some of the spiritual energy remains.

When I was there I picked up on three accidents (and by this I mean I sense things, though I'm not always given all the information of what happened), one of which occurred near what would have been an entrance – I felt it was in the area that is now the car park. I also picked up on several spirit energies. There was a happy man (a serviceman who was based there), another who'd been injured in an accident on this site (tragically, his legs had been blown off, although not the whole leg, just the lower part), and another sad man who'd transferred here from another base and then lost his life. They were two Englishmen and an American. I received the name Forbes psychically, as well as Bird. I feel Bird might have been a nickname for someone who was based there.

Further enquiries and research have revealed that there were many deaths at this location (and beyond, for a mile or so) during WWII, including planes coming down nearby and crashes at the site.

Although I received some names here, it is impossible to establish if they were the names of the spirits I sensed.

RAF Calshot – Hampshire

This is a wonderfully tranquil site located at the mouth of the Solent, and there are many layers of history here. Sitting proudly by the water's edge is King Henry VIII's Calshot Castle, built by the king as a defence to guard the entrance to Southampton. Located across the car park are some Aircraft Hangars from WWII, each named after planes. The site is now owned and managed by Hampshire County Council so is well maintained, and it doesn't really resemble a former RAF site.

Driving into the site takes you past the former Officers' Mess, a large building resembling a house that sits very close to the water's edge. Calshot also has a beach, a stretch of shingle popular with fishermen and families, as well as those who enjoy all manner of water sports. Spectacular views over to the Isle of Wight and along the coast to Portsmouth (Portsmouth's Spinnaker Tower is quite clearly visible from here) make this a spectacular day out.

Having picked up on some spirit energies almost immediately after parking my car, I soon set up my equipment, though unfortunately I couldn't make a long video as the battery on my camcorder was low. However, I did still have my PSB7 spirit box and voice recorder with me.

The PSB7 spirit box is a device roughly the size of a mobile phone, and it transmits instant, unexplained voices (known as Electronic Voice Phenomena, or EVPs), which seem to convey intelligence by referencing information relating to the location of a particular spirit. It works by scanning both FM and AM bands with a high-frequency accompaniment, such as white noise. Spirit beings are then able to use this white noise to form words for us to hear.

Anyway, I sat by the Sopwith Hangar, and after a few minutes – in my peripheral vision – I saw the spirit of a lady, seemingly in her early twenties and wearing a light-coloured uniform, walking towards the hangar. She was not aware of me. I sensed this was a 'time replaying ghost', the type we can't communicate with as it's like a snapshot of a movie, a replay of moving images that happened long ago.

I've come across this many, many times before. For some reason, when the time is right, the veil between the worlds becomes thinner (or is lifted somehow) and we get images and/ or sounds of times gone by. This was one of those images.

She walked with purpose, as if on a job that perhaps had a time scale and had to be completed urgently. Psychically, I heard the name Carol. The PSB7 picked up some quite audible words, including the reply 'RAF Calshot', when I asked where we were.

RAF Holmsley South – Bransgore, Hampshire

I visited this location, which is situated near a campsite in the New Forest, several times over an 18-month period. The first time, I went with my son on a warm summer's day, and we sat there in the evening as it started getting dark. There is a lovely memorial there, and we sat quietly on the bench within the little garden dedicated to those who lost their lives fighting for our freedom. For this investigation, I was using my camcorder with night vision as well as my EMF (electromagnetic field) detector.

Electromagnetic fields are always present all around us, and are invisible to the human eye. These are naturally forming energies, and spirit entities and ghosts can manipulate these frequencies, using them to initiate contact with sensitive people. This is why, when a person is having an experience that is considered paranormal, the air around them often feels charged – similar to how the atmosphere feels just before a thunderstorm.

Suddenly, my son and I both looked at each other, as we'd both heard a noise that was without doubt that of a Spitfire Engine. I knew that residential homes in nearby Southampton had been used to build these magnificent planes as well as other locations close by, and I later found out that they did indeed fly from here.

"Can you hear that?" my son asked.

"I can indeed," I replied, excited as the camera was recording at the time.

The sound lasted for about five seconds, and the camcorder had recorded it all – although it is more easily heard when listening to it through headphones.

A later visit, this time on my own, resulted in a rather different experience. It was dusk, and as it was February it was very cold – the temperature was -1°C. I sat down on a little memorial bench, and then I asked for spirit presences to draw close; I could sense they were around me again.

Before long I started hearing a noise over by the hedge behind the memorial – it was like a tapping sound. I was drawn to this noise so I went over to take a look, my camcorder recording my every movement.

Suddenly, to my left, I strongly felt the energy of a male soldier; it was almost enveloping me, like it was giving me an invisible hug. I sensed there was anger, not towards me but to a situation that occurred after the airfield was closed. I sensed this soldier had been based here, and that he'd continued to give service right up until its closure, but that he hadn't returned home. I picked up that he was from Canada and couldn't return home for some reason. His energy was incredibly strong.

Further research has revealed that there were several accidents at the airbase after it closed, although at the time of writing, I was unaware of these.

Woodchester Mansion – Nailsworth, Gloucestershire

Located in the beautiful Gloucestershire countryside, this Gothic mansion has a vibe all of its own. Approaching the mansion can be daunting as it lies at the end of a mile-long lane shrouded by dense woodland, the lane itself being allegedly haunted by WWII soldiers, Roman soldiers, a headless horseman, and a suicidal monk to name but a few.

Walking along the lane, one gets a sense of being watched – so common in these locations – as well as a feeling that the energy around you is changing, as if you're stepping into the past and then back out again into the present moment. I've experienced this at many locations, including Berry Pomeroy Castle, which is synonymous with time slip experiences. Woodchester Mansion is another location where this happens. The mansion, which was built on the site of an earlier house called Spring Park, has a long history stretching back thousands of years to the Roman occupation.

Walking around the ground floor, I was immediately drawn to the end of a corridor where there was an entrance to the church. I went inside. Due to building work, there was scaffolding all over, and because of this it was hard to see the real layout of the room, but even so there was a strong male presence around. I could feel that this man was a stern and foreboding character – not someone to mess with – and he immediately made me feel uncomfortable. I politely asked if I could speak with him telepathically, but this request was not welcomed.

His reaction was just something I could feel – I suddenly became uncomfortable, sensing that my energy wasn't welcomed here. People often find this hard to relate to, as in today's society we're not exactly encouraged to rely on our feelings; these days, it's all about logic. 40,000 years ago – when we used our instinct to hunt – it was all about feeling and sensing where prey was in order to survive. When I sense spirit entities, I use a similar approach to assess how they're feeling towards me.

When I wandered out into the corridor to take some photos the big heavy door slammed shut right behind me, sending me jumping into the air. I was soon joined by several other people, who'd come into the corridor to see what the huge bang was. I believe the presence I'd felt was the spirit of William Leigh, a Roman Catholic (and a previous owner of Woodchester Mansion) who perhaps was not at all open to the idea of mediums and psychics trying to communicate with him, no matter how polite they were!

Several of the photographs I took at this location contained orbs. These are small balls of energy, often translucent, and even coloured on rare occasions. They are said to be spirits manifesting in the first stages, and if one uses a camera that takes pictures in quick succession, these orbs can often be caught moving slowly across the room. Some people believe orbs in photos are just dust or insects or moisture on the lens, but I don't think so, especially when there's just one; a singular orb in a photo is more convincing to me than a photo containing lots of them.

A visit to the top corridor also yielded results. Every time I've visited here and have sat quietly at one end of the corridor, I've had the feeling of a male spirit rushing toward me in an aggressive way as if to say, 'Leave, Leave!'

Often in these situations I don't feel scared, as for the most part I'm able to rationalise what's happening; I am familiar with the effects of adrenaline and what it can do to us. It can definitely be unsettling to encounter something that appears to be overpowering and negative, but equally I recognise that we can give this feeling of terror so much power that it can build and build and quickly get out of hand. So, I have to keep any fear I might be feeling under control.

A trip into the basement of this wonderful house proved exciting and a little scary. I went into a room that had stone walls and sand on the floor – not thick sand, just a layer of fine grit with more stone underneath. While I was there, for some reason, I wanted to take a photo looking back up the corridor behind me. As I snapped two shots, the first showed a black mass against the wall whilst the other, taken immediately after, showed nothing on the wall whatsoever, though I hadn't moved at all. I quickly checked for any shadows being created by me, as there was a small window behind where I was standing, but that didn't explain the black mass. I didn't feel uncomfortable standing there, though I did feel as if I wasn't alone. Black masses have been reported floating in this area before, and I'm pretty sure I captured this black entity on camera.

A larger room in the basement proved uneventful, however, there have been many sightings in this location of a dwarf dating back to Roman times. The dwarf was a muse to the soldiers, a humorous plaything who also acted as a servant.

The grounds also have a spooky feel to them.

During WWII, both American and Canadian soldiers set up their base in the house, using the cellar to store equipment. One day, a terrible accident on the nearby lake led to the deaths of several soldiers who were taking part in a training exercise in preparation for D-Day; during the training exercise, the bridge that had been built over the lake collapsed, and sadly, several of the soldiers taking part in the exercise drowned. Their bodies were stored in the cellar.

A trip to the portable toilets erected for visitors also proved interesting; I went in to the cubicle and heard someone come in directly behind me – I heard the door open and close – but when I looked there was no one there.

A trip to this magnificent house is a must for anyone wishing to experience paranormal happenings. It's another place in the UK where the veil between this world and the next is thin.

Woodchester Mansion black mist © Alison Crocker

Ghostly Athelhampton – Dorset's most haunted house

Athelhampton (built in 1485 by Sir William Martyn) is one of the finest 15th century manor houses in the UK, and is surrounded by one of the great architectural gardens of England.

Dating from circa 1891, this Grade I listed garden is full of beautiful flowers, including the most magnificent magnolia I have ever seen, with flowers the size of my hand. The garden also has a dovecote dating back to the 15th century. A house with a long history is no stranger to all things paranormal.

One report that stands out at this location is of two men having a sword fight. The whole spectacle is said to have been witnessed by a woman sitting in the Great Hall as she quietly read a book. The two men have never been identified but the house is said to have connections to Royalists during the Civil War.

The wine cellar is said to experience tapping from an unknown source, and various owners, staff, and guests have all seen what can only be described as a Grey Lady. The current owner of Athelhampton, Mr Robert Cooke, has reported seeing her in the early hours, passing through the walls of the bedrooms.

One of the staff became aware of footsteps behind her in one of the corridors, and when she turned around, she saw – in broad daylight – a dark apparition that looked like a monk, standing outside the bathroom door. It is believed that this person was a Catholic priest.

Perhaps the most well-known ghost of them all is the pet ape, which was allegedly entombed in a secret passage behind the Great Chamber. Though the ghost has never been seen, you can often hear it scratching at the panels of the Great Chamber as it tries to escape.

When I visited, I was already familiar with this location as it had been used in one of *Most Haunted*'s very first episodes. I went to the corridor that team member Rick had refused to walk down, having been completely overcome with a feeling of terror and dread, though I personally didn't feel anything there. I did feel there had been some alteration to the staircase, and that this wasn't the original one, and I also very strongly sensed the presence of a lady in one of the bedrooms. She seemed to be from around the 18th century and was filled with sadness and a sense of loss. I also sensed the presence of a baby girl that passed here. I heard, clairaudiently, the name Caroline.

The cellar also had a vibe; although no tapping was heard here, I did get that all too familiar feeling that I wasn't alone. I also felt that someone had been locked in, perhaps for a joke or something, as I sensed the door slam shut behind me. This would be difficult, however, to verify.

Spectral Monk – Beaulieu, Hampshire

Whilst driving along a forest road between Brockenhurst and Beaulieu, I saw something light grey flit between some trees to my right. Moving closer, I saw a monk wearing a long white robe walking through the trees. He stood about 5ft 11, he had short white hair, and his robes were grey at the bottom due to them getting wet and muddy. I suspect he came from nearby Beaulieu Abbey, situated about a mile away.

Wymering Manor – Portsmouth, Hampshire

A few miles away from the centre of Portsmouth, the Grade II listed Wymering Manor sits on a small estate surrounded by modern-day homes. While a Roman settlement is located nearby, the house itself can be found on a site dating to around 1042.

Although the majority of the construction dates back to the 16th century, some Roman and medieval building materials have been found in parts of the manor, with the archaeology of the surrounding area implying the site has been inhabited since Roman times.

Once inside the manor, you are greeted by an enormous hall that is dominated by twin Jacobean staircases. The panelled walls are in the style associated with the Tudor Elizabethan period, and there are two priest holes located in the house.

During my visit, I remember sitting in complete darkness on an old sofa in the hall with my eyes on the two staircases, as I felt that someone or something was going to come down the stairs at any moment. Due to their use as portals between this world and the next, you'll often find that staircases are scenes of paranormal occurrences – this is one possible explanation as to why so many ghost sightings occur on staircases.

In 2003 – while the manor was a hostel – it was upgraded to a Grade II* listed building, quickly becoming a favourite venue for ghost hunters all across the UK. The hostel was eventually closed and the manor sold off by the council when the costs of looking after the building became too high; a timber support collapsed in 2006 and proved costly to repair. There have been plans to convert the manor into a hotel with function rooms, however at the time of writing the manor now belongs to the council. So, who haunts this enigmatic location?

When I spent the night in Wymering Manor, I sat in one of the rooms in total darkness, and when I glanced down at my hands and forearms they looked as if they were drenched in blood. This really freaked me out. I later found out that a ghostly nun is often seen wandering around the place with bloody hands – a gruesome image, but with an even more gruesome story behind it. As I learnt, illicit relations between monks and nuns meant that babies were often aborted and buried in the grounds of the house.

The manor is also allegedly connected to the Wymering church, and possibly even to Southwick Priory, by old tunnels that may have been used by local smugglers.

It is another location where I wouldn't want to need the bathroom in the middle of the night!

Fort Southwick – Portsmouth, Hampshire

Fort Southwick sits on Portsdown Hill, overlooking the naval city of Portsmouth. Construction on the fort began in 1861 and continued until its completion in 1870. Armed with 23 guns, it also housed a large water tank that supplied the neighbouring forts with water, as well as providing accommodation for around 220 men.

During the Second World War its tunnels were part of the secret communications nerve centre for Operation Overlord (the code name for the Battle of Normandy), with over a thousand people being stationed above ground at various headquarters associated with the D-Day planning.

The site remained in use until 1974, when the tunnels were abandoned.

I've investigated this location many times, two of which were all-night events. One night in particular, I decided to join a secondary group who were investigating another part of the extensive tunnels. Walking down the damp, dark tunnels that stretch on for miles is very unnerving, but still I began to walk alone down the tunnel with just a tiny flashlight for company.

To start with I was walking at a normal pace, though this quickly changed to a sprint when I absolutely *knew* I was being followed. Glancing behind me, there was nothing to see but pitch-blackness. That, plus the echo of my footsteps convincing me I could hear other steps, had me terrified; I've never been so glad to see the distant torchlight of the other group!

When investigating, all lights are turned off and the claustrophobic feeling is intense.

There are many spirits who haunt this location, including neighbouring Fort Widley. During that visit, a young drummer boy who I estimated to be around 17 years old, an older man who is always very drunk and abusive towards women, and even two cavaliers, were just some of the many spirit beings that myself and the other members of the group sensed around us.

I was also aware of a young boy watching me as I made my way through the damp darkness of the tunnel, but I felt that the main threat was from the older drunk man who liked to intimidate and scare unsuspecting visitors.

This intoxicated man has been witnessed by several other investigation groups in the past, so I already knew of his existence. He is quite a strong presence and his energy is rather dominating.

Durlston Country Park and Tilly Whim Caves – Swanage, Dorset

Dorset County Council are the proud owners of this beautiful castle that sits within a 280-acre park and nature reserve, an area that stretches along the coastline just south of Swanage. It is considered the gateway to the Jurassic Coast.

I spent two days at this location, taking with me my camcorder and spirit box, which are particularly useful on the coast as the water can act as an amplifier of spiritual energies.

Towards the end of the 18th century, the roof of Durlston Castle was used by the communications pioneer Marconi when engineers were working on strengthening the signal of radio transmissions from the south coast across to the Isle of Wight.

Sitting quietly on the cliff top, I tuned into the spirit world and switched on my spirit box. It was actually quite active, and immediately I clearly heard several words that were related to telecommunications. I didn't know about the Marconi connection until I listened back to the footage later at home and did some internet research.

Standing on a cliff top near the lighthouse, I was very aware of a spirit energy that had passed at this spot, and in that moment I was filled with the strangest sensation of wanting to jump off the cliff and onto the rocks below. Before the Anvil Point Lighthouse was built in 1881, this area would have seen many ships break up as they hit the rocks in the dark. I sensed people anxiously awaiting the arrival of rescuers, while relatives of the rescuers were waiting to see them come home safely.

Knowlton Church – Wimborne, Dorset

Built in the 12th century, Knowlton Church is surrounded by a Neolithic ritual henge earthwork (a particular type of earthwork from the Neolithic period, typically consisting of a circular shaped bank with an internal ditch), and due to the unfamiliar pairing of the henge and the church (symbolising the change from Pagan to Christian worship) it has a rather strange vibe to it.

When it was built it was formed using stone and flint, and although now just a ruin, it is easy to imagine how the church would have looked all those centuries ago.

As I live quite close to this location I have been able to visit many times, both during the day and at night. Various spectres have been seen here: a tall man in a long dark cloak, misty humanoid shapes, and floating candles, which have been seen where windows would once have been. During some of my visits I haven't felt comfortable at all, resulting in me leaving hastily, whereas other times I've felt quite peaceful and have wanted to stay.

As with so many of these historical places, the all too familiar sense of foreboding is always present. The church is situated on a main ley line, linking it to both Glastonbury (approx. 50 miles to the south-west) and Stonehenge (approx. 27 miles north), and we must not forget that these lines can amplify spiritual happenings when the conditions are right.

Several years ago, when on a night-time vigil with a group of people, I found myself constantly looking up to the sky.

I could clearly hear the words 'as above so below' in my mind, and I took this to mean there was a mysterious link between the stars and this location.

Some years later I heard the story of a person who, when visiting the ruin, had an encounter with two alien beings as well as witnessing a UFO. The full account of this fantastic interaction has been detailed in Roger Guttridge's book, *Paranormal Dorset*.

Nothe Fort – Weymouth, Dorset

This coastal defence, shaped like the letter D, was built between 1860 and 1872 to protect Portland and Weymouth Harbours, though it was abandoned in 1956. Having been purchased by the local council in 1961, it is now a museum.

The main fort has been Grade II* listed since 1974, and according to a 2007 study conducted by The National Lottery, it was voted one of the 'spookiest' locations in the UK.

I investigated Nothe Fort in 2012, when I joined a fee-paying investigation group. Unbeknownst to me at the time, the party consisted of stags and hens aged around 25, many of whom were 'three sheets to the wind' before the event had even started, due to a pre-investigation visit to a local pub! Needless to say, a few hours into the investigation I knew I had made a mistake and decided to break away from the group and 'go it alone'.

My spirit encounter in the café area was with a young soldier from the late 1800s, who communicated with me through whistling – I feel he would have had the nickname Whistler. Sitting alone in the dark I was able to clearly hear the distant sound of doors banging, though I cannot be sure if this was down to the rest of the group or something otherworldly.

I took some amazing photos in the nuclear bunker – a sealed room within the fort that had a rather unusual atmosphere. I do wonder if this atmosphere could be attributed to infrasound, where sound waves are lower than human audibility, as these are 'felt' rather than heard.

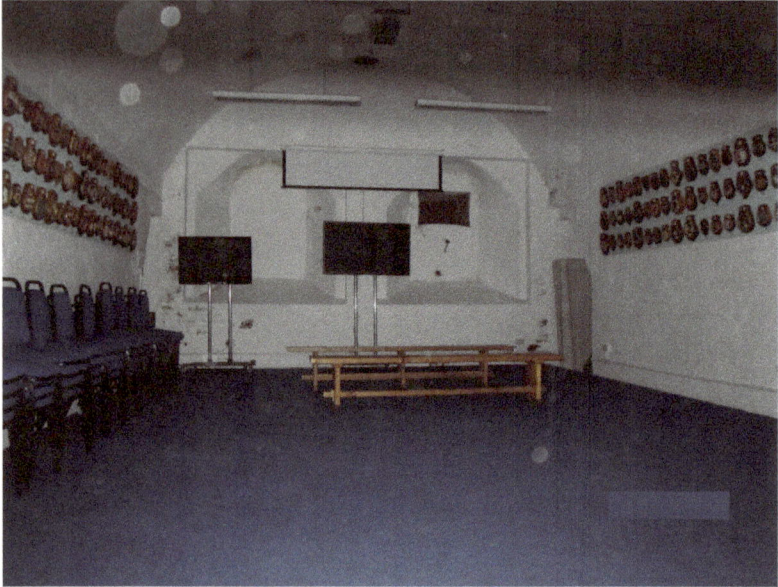

Many orbs caught in the nuclear bunker at Nothe Fort © Alison Crocker

Highgate Cemetery – London

Having grown up in the 1970s, and therefore having spent many nights watching *Hammer House of Horror* movies, I knew that Highgate Cemetery (which opened in 1839) had been used in the production of some of these British-made classics. There is a part of this beautifully haunting place called the Circle of Lebanon, which is an avenue of classical-style tombs located in the western part of the cemetery, and many spectres have been seen here. Rumours of a vampire, a floating man in Victorian clothing, and the charred remains of a headless woman have all made an appearance over the years.

I had longed to visit this place for many years, and a couple of years ago I decided to make the journey to north London so I could have a walk around and see if I could pick up any energies.

Walking around the perimeter fence I was immediately aware of many spirit beings, and I was soon experiencing the familiar feeling of being around some not so pleasant energies.

Once inside the cemetery, I immediately saw (clairvoyantly) a young lady wearing a long white dress that appeared to date back to around the 1800s, dashing around the stones in a rather demented way. She seemed to be in her early twenties and I felt she had suffered with psychiatric difficulties for most of her short life. I saw her several times during my visit, flitting in between the stones, shrieking and kneeling at random graves, and praying wildly.

This woman is the perfect example of a 'time replaying ghost' – ghosts who come and go as opposed to a grounded spirit. She was flitting around the gravestones because this was what she did in her lifetime – this was her usual behaviour. I didn't feel scared by her as she had no idea I was there; she was not a spirit one could communicate with, because it was just the imprint of her energy that I was witnessing. For this reason, it would not have been possible to rescue her. She was a ghost rather than a spirit, and as ghosts are just time replaying energies, we cannot communicate or connect with them in any way.

A few months later I received a message via my website from the Highgate Vampire Appreciation Society confirming that this young lady's ghost had indeed been seen by other visitors over the years.

Berry Pomeroy Castle –
Totnes, Devon

This castle and its grounds are one of my favourite locations. I've visited dozens of times, each time experiencing something different from the last.

The first time I went I met a fellow dowser called Bob who, as a local man, visited the castle regularly to dowse for spirits. It was at this location that I had what I can only describe as a time slip experience. This is where time distorts somehow and for a short time you travel back to another year, experiencing what life would have looked like back then.

My experience occurred in the grounds. Bob and I had gone for a walk, down the pathway that leads to the valley at the foot of the hill on which this majestic ruined castle stands. There is a small cottage there and as we walked past it, Bob noticed that the birds had stopped singing. We had previously been enjoying a warm spring day with the usual springtime birdsong clearly audible, but now they fell silent. Looking around us, we also noticed that everything had taken on a strange shimmering appearance, similar to the effect that occurs when holograms appear in the *Star Wars* movies.

Looking at the cottage, we noticed that there were no curtains at the windows, and an old-fashioned laundry mangle sat on a rickety table outside. There was also a strange-looking plant in the garden that Bob didn't recognise, which was unusual as he was a keen gardener. The whole place just looked like something out of the 1800s. We were also both overcome by a strange eerie feeling, similar to what I'd experienced during the total eclipse back in 1999.

This whole episode lasted less than a minute, after which normality returned, the birds started singing again, and this time when we looked at the cottage, we saw there were both net curtains and lined curtains at the windows. The mangle was still there, but we wondered if it had been placed outside as some kind of museum piece.

I read some time later that a local light aircraft pilot had once flown over the castle and seen chimney smoke billowing from the roof that he knew had long since gone.

Corfe Castle – Dorset

Since it was built 1000 years ago, Corfe Castle has had a rich and colourful history, the building changing from a royal fortress to a private residence, and finally, to a National Trust property. It has been a defensive site, as well as the location of a six week-long siege, and has also fallen to Parliamentary sappers, who brought the towers and ramparts down with gunpowder.

One warm spring day in May 2014 I decided to visit Corfe Castle, a small village in rural Dorset named after the castle of the same name, and due to the weather and the scenery, there were quite a few people milling about.

I have always been in awe of the castle, having found a painting of it at a car boot sale decades earlier and being immediately taken in by its charm and the way the castle's perched on a strange pointed hill in between two others. I knew of its paranormal occurrences but didn't have any details. I did know, however, that flickering lights had been seen in the ramparts as well as the sound of a gate opening and closing when no one's around.

I was walking down a corridor and under an arch when, suddenly, a large rock came tumbling down from above, almost striking the German tourist who stood about a foot away from me! He turned to me and glared as if to say, 'Why did you throw that?' and I said, "It wasn't me, I didn't throw it!" while holding my hands in the air as if to say 'I'm clueless!' He looked back at me and I could clearly see he didn't believe me.

He wandered off, and I picked the rock up from the floor – it must have weighed at least two pounds. I then looked up to where I thought the rock had fallen from and saw that it was just a wall. There was no level above or anywhere where someone could stand.

If it had hit anyone, that rock could have really hurt them – or worse.

This incident really shook me up, so I walked back to the castle entrance and found a castle guide, telling them all about it.

The guide seemed quite interested, but suggested that perhaps a bird had been carrying the rock and dropped it, as it was currently nesting time. I don't think this was possible; the bird would have to have been the size and strength of a Golden Eagle to carry something that large and heavy!

I think this was a spirit, perhaps trying to get attention. I believe if they have something to say they will find any means to be heard.

Bigfoot Sighting – Wilton, Salisbury, Wiltshire

Back in 2014 on the night of a full moon, a group of friends decided to investigate some woods just north of Salisbury. Grovely Wood is one of the largest woodlands in southern Wiltshire, and both Iron Age and Roman archaeology still exist there, with a Roman road running through the wood from East to West.

Whilst in these mysterious woods (having already walked quite some distance in), the group heard the sounds of snapping twigs, heavy footsteps, and stones being thrown. On top of this, two members of the group reported seeing a 9ft hairy humanoid come at them from behind some trees. The witness who contacted me also told me that after her visit to the woods, she went on to experience intense headaches for six weeks, as well as a feeling of something 'probing' inside her head. These pains were accompanied by strange dreams.

More than twenty years ago, I went horse riding in these woods with a group, and was unfortunate enough to be the one at the back of the line. I did not feel at all comfortable throughout the whole hour's ride; my horse was skittish (did it sense something too?) and I also had the overpowering feeling that I was being watched.

Cley Hill – Warminster, Wiltshire

Cley Hill is a prominent hill to the west of Warminster in Wiltshire, England, located on 66 acres of land owned by the National Trust. If you are able to walk up the very steep hill, you are rewarded with a wonderful view. Archaeological features include a large Iron Age hill fort, two bowl barrows (mounds of earth), and medieval strip lynchets – terraced sections of earth seen on hillsides.

I visited several years ago, having already known of its history in relation to the Warminster Thing (a series of UFO sightings and associated phenomena relating to UFOs that took place in the area) back in the 1960s. Strange aerial sightings are still being observed today, with an interesting video featuring a UFO appearing in the media as recently as 2017.

I received this account from someone who wishes to remain anonymous. The witness described seeing a disc with what looked like hieroglyphic symbols on it flying off towards Cley Hill at around 8 pm on an evening in April 1997. The person reports that they found the whole thing traumatising.

I visited a few years ago to see if I could be another one of the many people to report seeing something unusual here. Climbing up to the top of the hill, I saw the apparition of a small man (around 3ft 6) about 200 metres away from me, wearing sackcloth rags. There was also something on his head, which didn't look like a hat as such, but rather some kind of covering. I wasn't scared; it was the middle of the afternoon and I didn't feel threatened at all. It was just a curious sighting.

Big Cat Sightings

Whilst driving on the A338 through a hamlet in Wiltshire called Britford (which has minimal streetlighting), a large cat startled me by suddenly running out in front of my car, leaping from right to left, and clearing the road in three 'bounds'. It was enormous – it's hard to be precise but I would say it was about the size of a German Shepherd with a very long tail (about 2.5 feet) in length. It was completely black with glowing amber/yellow eyes.

During that same year, I received two other sightings of a similar creature in the same area (within a five-mile radius of Salisbury), and as these sightings were by completely unrelated witnesses, I believe it was the same creature.

Twelve miles south of this location, I received another witness account from someone living at Rockford Common – an area close to Ringwood in Hampshire – who also saw a large black cat.

Ball of Light UFO, Sixpenny Handley – Dorset

This account was given to me by two friends in 1990, when they were out messing around in their cars. I know both young men personally and I can vouch for their credibility and honesty.

There is a lonely stretch of road between Cranborne and Sixpenny Handley, one that is very close to a Roman Road, which is clearly visible from the main road. There are no streetlights and only the odd house dotted here and there, separated by miles of rolling Dorset hills.

The two boys, who were out in separate cars, decided to pull into a lay-by on the side of the road next to some woods, to smoke some cigarettes and generally have a chat. Drawing up alongside each other, their cars facing the deep, dark wooded area, one of the boys saw a small ball of yellow-coloured light flitting in and out of the trees at a distance of about 200 metres. On mentioning this to his friend, he saw it too, and they both sat in silence as they watched this ball move slowly towards them in an unusual swaying motion. They wondered if it was someone carrying a lantern as the size of lantern light would have fit what they were seeing, but they couldn't see a person; the ball of light just seemed to be floating about six feet from the ground.

Mesmerised, they continued to watch until it was about 50 metres away from their cars. By now, the boys both admit to being scared. There was no sound, no twig snap, only the quiet rustling of the trees gently swaying. Rather hurriedly, they decided to leave.

Jelly-like UFO – Poole, Dorset, and Salisbury, Wiltshire

I was given this report second-hand about someone enjoying the night sky whilst smoking a cigarette in the summer of 2014. The witness reports seeing something large 'flapping' quite high up, leaving a wiggly lined vapour behind it as it went. It appeared transparent, like jelly, and looked completely surreal.

This is interesting to me in particular because, over the past few years, I have seen something very similar to this from my home in Wiltshire. My house is situated on a hill and the area of sky where I witnessed this phenomenon was strangely in the direction of Poole (the same area as the other witness account), some 25 miles south-west. I tried to describe this to my son who is a keen astronomer, and he struggled to find an explanation. Whatever it was, it was quite big. I held my arm up so the night sky became a backdrop, and this 'thing' was about the size of that, so in comparison, it was quite enormous – 60 degrees wide in astronomical terms.

Ghost – Rufus Stone, New Forest, Hampshire – a witness account

Me and a mate were driving through the New Forest one night when, wanting to get some rest, we parked up to sleep in the car. We both saw a will-o'-the-wisp (a pale-coloured flame or phosphorescence that is sometimes seen over wet and boggy ground at night) but didn't think much of it. When we woke the next morning, we saw we were next to the Rufus Stone. This was about 25 years ago. I don't know if it is signposted or if you can park there now but we had no idea. I didn't know until now that it was supposed to be haunted but it looks like we saw a ghost!

Royal Victoria Country Park – Southampton, Hampshire

Once the site of the world's largest military hospital, this enigmatic location – which opened to the public as a 200-acre park in 1970 – has seen many spooky happenings over the years. Today, all that remains of the hospital is the chapel, which now acts as a heritage centre with a 150-foot-high viewing tower.

The surrounding woods also have an eerie feel to them, with the 4000-grave military cemetery definitely adding to the ghostly feeling.

A witness called Simon emailed me with an account of when he and a friend saw a big cat at this location. A friend of mine once saw a tall hooded figure moving slowly in and out of the trees as he sat in his car with his girlfriend. This figure was a pure black mass, and seemed to be hovering along above the ground. My friend was terrified as he sped out of the car park and towards the safety of town!

Ghost on bridge at Poole Railway Station

Walking over the bridge, I strongly sensed the sad presence of a young girl, aged around 12, wearing a white smock-type dress typical of the Victorian era. She died either at this location or very close by.

Lymington Shop – Lymington, Hampshire

Ten years ago, I went to the book section of a new age shop in Lymington. This shop was a real gem, featuring three floors of new age goods, incense, cushions, wall plaques, candles, and more. The whole shop was quite a size, and steeped in history – its stone walls dated back to the 1700s at least.

The book section was right at the back of the shop, and as I made my way there, I became immediately aware of a dark energy near me, as well as a feeling of something not very pleasant; I instantly felt cold and unwelcome. I walked out of the book section and through the shop to the person at the cashier's desk, asking if she knew whether or not the shop was haunted.

She replied, rather stiffly, that she had recently paid someone to 'get rid' of the ghost that haunts that section of the shop and seemed to take offence that I had even brought the subject up. Feeling awkward, I bought some items – including some books – and left.

Highcliffe Castle - Dorset

This once ruined castle has long been a place of wonderment for me. I first went to see it around 1976, when it was just a burnt-out shell, sealed off from vandals (rather unsuccessfully) by high fences; two fires over the years had completely destroyed it. All this changed in 1998 when the Heritage Lottery fund agreed to pay £2.6 million to begin the long and arduous task of restoring this magnificent building back to its former glory.

Another visit around 2005 proved quite lucky for me. After I'd spent some time chatting with a very helpful castle guide, he offered – providing I was prepared to wear a hard hat – to take me around the part of the castle that had not yet seen any renovations or visitors.

We entered the castle via a small door that led into the basement. It was dark, dank, and spooky. Walking along the narrow corridor in partial darkness, I became immediately aware of the spirits of children and one boy in particular, aged around six or seven, who was small, fragile, and perhaps disabled. With this child, I immediately sensed that there had been some kind of abuse going on here when the castle had been a children's home from 1950 to 1952. I sensed that unspeakable things had gone on and that they'd been covered up, especially one incident in particular in 1952 concerning alleged child abuse.

I mentioned my feelings to the guide, who informed me that it had indeed been a children's home, although I didn't know that at the time.

In 2008 I received an invitation from a paranormal group to attend a paranormal investigation at the castle. By this time, a lot of restoration work had taken place and it was possible to walk around the ground floor areas with ease. The former dining room proved eerie, especially with the alleged tale of a security guard's dog wetting itself with fear on entering the dining room and refusing to go in thereafter.

During the night, a walk around the woods surrounding the castle also proved interesting as I picked up on many US soldiers who'd been located there in WWII. I found out later that was indeed accurate; many US troops were there because the western end of the nearby cliff top nature reserve was attained by the MOD, and had become involved in secret radar and signals intelligence.

As I made my way through the grounds I saw, walking towards me, the spirit of a lady, just as I heard the words 'Australia' and '1926' in my head. In my mind's eye I was shown images of a lady singing, but I had no idea what this could mean. I then realised that the lady walking towards me – wearing a fitted black velvet top and pale skirts – was an opera singer from Australia. I had to find out who she was and why she was visiting the castle!

My research at home uncovered that I had seen the apparition of Dame Nellie Melba, an Australian opera singer who had visited the castle in 1926 on what was to have been her last visit to Europe before her death in 1931. She had been an old friend of the castle's owner at that time.

RAF Stoney Cross – Hampshire

RAF Stoney Cross is a former World War II airfield located 4 miles (6.4 km) northwest of Lyndhurst and 12 miles (19 km) west of Southampton, the remains sitting on the New Forest Crown land.

When it was in use (from 1942 to 1948), it served both the Royal Air Force and the United States Army Air Forces, functioning primarily as a combat bomber and fighter airfield.

Myself and my sons visited this location over a few nights, and I found many spiritual presences here. We took with us our EMF reader, which can sometimes be useful in investigations because they detect the alterations in the electromagnetic field surrounding us. Humans give off 0.2 milligauss, and whenever paranormal events are happening, EMF readers detect changes ranging from between 2 and 6 milligauss. During our time here, we believe we caught spiritual lights, which are different to orbs; they appear as tiny pinpricks of light, often in our peripheral vision, which is more sensitive.

I sensed the spirit of a serviceman called Jonny, as well as that of someone with the nickname Sneezy or Sneezer. We also believe we caught on camera the outline of a ghost car or vehicle, and I sensed that there had been some kind of accident at the airfield involving military vehicles. It was a creepy night and all of us heard the sound of twigs snapping very close to us.

As I was writing this, I received the following witness account regarding RAF Stoney Cross, which confirms what I sensed when I was there:

'I am not particularly interested in the paranormal, though I do believe that there are 'things' out there and I do believe that

there are people, like yourself, who can communicate with spirits, if that is what they are.

My interest in Stoney Cross airfield is predominantly historical. In the last six months – whilst working at the Ocknell and Longbeech campsite, which forms part of the former RAF Stoney Cross – I have carried out quite a bit of research into the history of the former airfield. Part of my duties were to conduct night-time closure patrols and the locking of not only the barrier at Ocknell, but also the road access gates onto Forest Road.

I am an ex-soldier and the majority of my patrols were undertaken without the use of any lights (I believe I can see better in the dark, whereas anyone showing a light would be easily seen). Now, there were times when I moved around the site when I could sense a distinct change in the atmosphere – a slight change of temperature, perhaps – and a feeling that there was 'something' there. Unexplainable! Not scary either, but the hairs on the back of my neck certainly went up!

During the course of my research, I have been able to gain the full architects' drawings for the airfield, which show all the buildings concerned, including the building designations. I was able to see from your description of Stoney Cross that you were down in the area near Fritham, in the North Bentley Inclosure. From my drawings, I can see that there was an aircraft dispersal point there, as well as maintenance buildings.

From a factual point of view, the airfield was built by Wimpey (yes, the same Taylor Wimpey that builds houses today), and there is an account on record of an accident that occurred there in 1942. This involved an aircraft (a P50 Mustang), which ran into a contractor's vehicle on the taxiway, killing the three occupants.'

Bigfoot and the Rune Connection

ISA   YOLE   GEBO

Rune Stones © Yana Pavlova

Rune stones are small pebbles with symbols written on them, and they date back to the times of the Vikings, when they were used as a method of communication; before the adoption of the Latin alphabet, runic alphabets were used to write various Germanic languages.

The earliest can be dated back to 150 AD, though by around 700-1100 AD most European cultures had replaced runic alphabets with the Latin alphabet. Runes were still used after this, however, for decorative or specialised purposes.

I wonder about the connection between these symbols and Bigfoot. This is because people have sent me photographs taken where suspected Bigfoot activity has taken place, featuring things (such as sticks and branches laid out in particular ways) that closely resemble these rune symbols.

Personally, I have seen a singular stick in the ground, which bears a striking resemblance to the sign I or Isa in the Rune language. Isa can be interpreted to mean ice or frozen, so a time to stand still and take stock, a time when we leave things as they are, frozen without movement. I have also seen branches and sticks in the sign of an X, which means Gyfu or gift, an offering. Another commonly used symbol found is Y, Yole, which refers to intuition, that inner knowing of what is going to happen, and trusting our inner feelings.

Are these Bigfoot creatures relying on an ancient method of communication between themselves and us, the mystified humans that perhaps have lost touch with this part of ourselves? The part that looks for signs and symbols in our everyday lives, using these clues either as a way of receiving answers that elude us or as a way of solving complex problems?

Burley and the Cone of Power

Mention the village of Burley to anyone familiar with the esoteric and the mystical and they will mention witchcraft – this tiny New Forest village was made famous by local celebrity and psychic Sybil Leek, who was once named the world's most famous witch by the BBC!

However, there is another name synonymous with this mysterious village: Gerald Gardner (1884 – 1964), who is considered by many as the person responsible for forming a new type of contemporary Pagan religion called Wicca.

Retiring as a civil servant in 1936, he soon became involved in cultivating the new religion, combining several ideas borrowed from Freemasonry and Ceremonial magic.

As Gerald lived nearby in Highcliffe, Dorset, he joined a coven of witches who were based in the New Forest, and it is in the woods that surround Burley that he and the other coven members created a most powerful ritual called 'Operation Cone of Power' in 1940. The aim of this ritual was to use magical energies to prevent the Nazis from invading England.

One August night, he and the others created a magic circle with a 'cone' of energy, sending the cone to Berlin along with the chant: 'you cannot come here, you cannot enter, you cannot cross the sea,' repeated over and over again.

So powerful was this ritual, it is thought that some of the older, frailer members of the coven fell to their knees during the ritual, sadly passing away soon after.

Netley Abbey – Southampton, Hampshire

Netley Abbey, founded in 1239 as a house for Cistercian monks, is located in the small village of Netley, on the outskirts of Southampton. After being seized by Henry VIII in 1536, it was given to William Paulet, who transformed the abbey into a mansion.

Since being abandoned and partially demolished, the ruins of the abbey became a bit of a tourist attraction, and now it (the church, cloister buildings, part of the mansion, and the abbot's house) is a scheduled monument, looked after by English Heritage.

There have been several strange tales regarding the abbey over the years, the main one being the story of Walter Taylor. He was a builder, and when he was contracted to demolish the church, it is said he had a dream – a dream where he started demolishing the building, and a part of it fell on him and killed him. He was worried this might be an omen, but after a friend told him to dismiss it, that's exactly what he did; he put the dream out of his mind and continued with the demolition – during which, he died. A part of the building fell on him, fracturing his skull and eventually killing him. Just like in his dream.

In 2004 I joined an all-night investigation at the abbey with *Most Haunted*'s Parapsychologist, Jason Karl. It was to prove to be a very interesting event.

In the enormous nave, around fifteen of us stood whilst a small group attempted a basic form of Gregorian chanting. This was suggested as an idea to invoke a reaction from the spirit realms, as it was imagined that the chanting may have been part of the daily lives of the monks.

After a few minutes – to the whole group's amazement, as we stood there, awestruck – we all witnessed the shadowy outlines of at least fifty monks moving slowly down the nave, floating away from us. It was truly incredible. Some of the group commented on how the nave no longer felt like a ruin, as if – for a few moments, at least – it had been brought back to life, giving us all a snapshot of the abbey's history.

As the chanting ceased, the shadowy monks seemed to evaporate and the nave returned to the present time.

Our next investigation was in the abbot's house. This was very uncomfortable, as I immediately sensed the menacing energy of a man who, when alive, would have been powerful and feared. Whilst standing in a circle, holding hands in complete darkness (with no torches), I immediately felt two hands on my back and then a violent push. I fell forward into the group and quickly spun around to see who had pushed me. There was no one there and I immediately knew this was the work of the abbot.

Later, in another part of the abbey (again in darkness), I watched as a black human shape moved slowly past the window. As the familiar feeling of a black cloud descended on the group, I knew this was the abbot again. At the same time, nearly all of the females in the group started complaining of stomach pains so bad that many were bending over double, in a highly distressed state – including me. I feel this was because somewhere in the abbey's long history a murder had taken place, when someone had been repeatedly stabbed. Fortunately, removing ourselves from that part of the abbey seemed to alleviate these horrible symptoms. I'd not seen this before, or since, where so many people are affected in one place by a spirit entity; it indicates the powerful energy that is always present here.

This night remains one of the most shocking and exhausting I've ever encountered, and it affected me deeply; I didn't say a word throughout the whole journey home and I even slept with a light on for weeks afterwards!

After many accounts of distress from other groups who attended after ours in 2004, English Heritage (who own this property) have banned paranormal groups from the premises at night on Health and Safety grounds.

The Bartley Thing - Hampshire

In the Summer of 2012 whilst sitting in my car enjoying an ice cream and reading a local magazine outside a shop in the tiny village of Bartley, Hampshire, I became aware of something on my right, moving slowly towards me. Looking up I saw a humanoid shape in excess of seven tall wearing a long purple and gold cloak with what looked like a golden crown on its head. I felt this thing was male but there was something about its face. It looked like a white mask and its beard looked like it was made of plastic. Ginger coloured hair poked out at the sides. The shape had no arms and legs and appeared to glide past my car until it was alongside the driver's door, some four feet from me, when it suddenly vanished.

I wasn't frightened by what I saw but had a strange feeling of gratitude, as if I should be grateful for seeing what had just 'floated' by. It was as if I was in the presence of something wonderful.

What is more curious about this story is I have never visited this village before. I've had no reason to. I just felt compelled to visit on that day and have not returned since. As if I had to be there to witness what I saw.

RESOURCES

Opening up to the Spirit World – a guided meditation

Welcome to this guided meditation designed to help you connect with spirit energies. I suggest you record yourself saying this out loud as it can be more powerful to hear our own voices than to listen to someone else's. It also adds value to your commitment to connect with the other side.

Before I start, please make sure that all mobile devices and computers near you are switched off and that you are in a place where you're not likely to be disturbed.

Allow yourself a few minutes to calm your thoughts and focus your breathing. You may sit or lie down, and it might be a good idea to have a warm blanket to cover you.

When you are comfortable, close your eyes and take three deep breaths, inhaling gently through your nose and then exhaling through your mouth.

Begin by visualising yourself enveloped in a bubble of white light. This glorious light begins as a star above your head and travels all the way down to your feet. See the light and know that this light is from the Divine Cosmos. It is protecting you, and by being protected by this light, your energy will only align with positive, helpful energies.

Take your focus to the top of your head, feeling your scalp relax, and then move this wonderful feeling of relaxation to your forehead, the tiny muscles around your eyes, and your cheeks. As you do this, you will feel all the tension melt away. Take note of how your jaw relaxes, then your neck and your shoulders. Notice how your arms feel heavy as you sink lower into the chair or bed, and how this relaxing feeling goes right out to the tips of your fingers. Take your awareness to your chest, tummy, and bottom, feeling as they relax and sink down. Be aware of how your legs feel so much heavier now they are relaxed. Your knees also feel heavy, and you can take this lovely heavy relaxed feeling all the way down to your toes. You feel so relaxed as you sink into the chair or bed. You are now fully relaxed, warm and comfortable.

Next, take your awareness to the top of your head, to your Crown Chakra, the chakra we use to receive messages from the spirit world. Visualise this area opening. Some people imagine a lotus flower slowly opening its bud, while others might see a doorway, ornately decorated or plain – it doesn't matter, just visualise what feels right for you. Once this chakra is fully open, take your attention to the area in the centre of your forehead. This is where your third eye is located. Your third eye is what enables you to 'see' clairvoyantly. Again, open this area in the method you have chosen.

Spend a few minutes receiving guidance. Use your thoughts to ask questions and listen to the replies you receive.

When you have finished, once more take your awareness to the top of your head and imagine your Crown Chakra closing. If it's a door, gently close the door, giving thanks as you do so. If it's a flower bud, see the petals gently closing one by one. Then, do the same with your third eye. Lastly, give blessings to the spirit world for any messages and guidance you received.

Psychic ability takes practice, so you should try to do this for 10-20 minutes every day. You may struggle at first but remember that we are all psychic, and that if we believe we are not, it's because we've been listening solely to the conscious mind, and perhaps other people who've told us this is nonsense.

How to see phantoms and mystical creatures

We don't have to summon up spirits at séances or spend money going on ghost hunts with a bunch of strangers to connect with the spirit world; sometimes people see things when they're not expecting to see anything. I believe that when this happens it is a nudge from our higher selves, telling us we need to start paying more attention to the spiritual and psychic aspects that are within all of us.

The most psychic times of the day are early morning and sunset. Personally, I've seen more ghosts in the daytime than I ever have at night.

Find somewhere that many people have walked, like a park or other open space; if possible, try to find somewhere that hasn't been heavily worked and where industrial changes haven't been made. A good place would be a castle or standing stone, as these places (such as Corfe Castle in Dorset and Lewes Castle in East Sussex) are usually surrounded by natural energies, although this doesn't always follow; I once had a ghostly encounter in a public toilet in Oxford City Centre!

Once you've found the right place, sit quietly for a few minutes, feeling your feet making contact with the Earth. Take some deep breaths and gently half-close your eyes. For more of a connection, hold a stone or twig taken from the place and as you hold the item, start to let images form in your mind. You may become aware of colours, hear sounds, and notice distinctive smells. You may also hear music from far away, as if it's being carried on the breeze.

You may become aware of a shadowy form in front of you, or of small pinpricks of light in your peripheral vision. These little lights are always spirit beings making their presence known.

Try to remember everything you feel, sense, and see. Psychic impressions may come to you randomly, and sometimes our psychic senses will show us certain images that we have to interpret. Usually, there will be a reason for these seemingly random images that will mean something to us personally.

Depending on where you are on your own spiritual path – whether you're just beginning or have been doing this for a while – try to understand that these symbols may have been sent as a trigger, encouraging you to dig deeper and go further within, something that will benefit you greatly.

Please try to understand that there is a higher purpose to all our lives and that nothing ever happens without good reason, although we don't always feel that at the time.

Try not to be disappointed if you didn't have a full-blown manifestation, as this isn't a test of your psychic abilities; this is just the beginning – or the expansion – of your current knowledge. When you leave, silently thank the spirits of the place, and if you did take a twig or rock from the place, please remember to return it before you go.

Past Life Regression – a guided session

To benefit fully from this guided meditation, I suggest you record it yourself using a voice recorder, perhaps on a phone or suchlike. Your own voice can be a very good way to assist in self-development as you are giving positive energy to it and acknowledging your own power.

Welcome to your personal past life regression session. Today, I am going to guide you to a past life that perhaps has a message for you for this current lifetime. This process can be enormously rewarding, offering comfort and answers to thoughts and feelings that perhaps have been stuck at the back of your mind, perhaps even for a long time.

First, it is important to make sure that you won't be disturbed for about 20-30 minutes. So, switch off all mobile devices, make sure your surroundings are safe, and find your-self a comfortable place in which to relax, such as a comfy chair or a bed. It may be a good idea to have a light blanket to cover you.

When you know it is safe to fully relax, take three deep breaths. Breathe in slowly through your nose and then exhale slowly through your mouth. As you do so you will feel the tension begin to melt away as you connect with the inner part of you, your soul, your spirit – that deep part of you that is with you always.

Take your focus to the top of your head, feeling your scalp relax, and then move this wonderful feeling of relaxation to your forehead, the tiny muscles around your eyes, and your cheeks. As you do this, you will feel all the tension melt away.

Take note of how your jaw relaxes, then your neck and your shoulders. Notice how your arms feel heavy as you sink lower into the chair or bed, and how this relaxing feeling goes right out to the tips of your fingers. Take your awareness to your chest, tummy, and bottom, feeling as they relax and sink down. Be aware of how your legs feel so much heavier now they are relaxed. Your knees also feel heavy, and you can take this lovely heavy relaxed feeling all the way down to your toes. You feel so relaxed as you sink into the chair or bed. You are now fully relaxed, warm and comfortable.

In your mind, visualise that you are at the top of a spiral staircase. Your intuition tells you that you must go down the spiral staircase because this will lead you to a past life, one that has a message for you. You also know that the further you go down the stairs, the more relaxed you will become. You take the first steps and begin to relax further, going deeper and becoming more relaxed. Notice that with each step you take down you feel so much more relaxed than before, going deeper and relaxing further.

As you reach the bottom step you feel that gloriously heavy relaxed feeling throughout your entire body. Before you, you see a long corridor. It is lit by candles, which give a warm, yellowy glow to your surroundings. You become aware that you are there to learn something important, and know that discovering this past life will offer up guidance and solutions to any niggling problems or challenges you have right now. Know that this special place always waits for you and is always there should you need it.

There are various doors along this corridor, and as you slowly move along, you look at each door. Your inner knowing is guiding you to the door that has your past life behind it. You are drawn to one particular door. You notice how it 'speaks' to you. You open the door and step into your past life, which has an important message for you in this lifetime. Where are you? What year is it? Are you male or female? In your mind, ask your higher self to be given answers to any questions you might have. Is there anyone who can assist you with your challenges? Trust that is all done by just allowing the thoughts to come. I'll stop talking now so you can listen to the message that is meant for you.

[Pause for several minutes.]

Now that you have the answers you seek; it is time for you to leave your past life.

You see the door you came through appearing in front of you. You step through the door and into the corridor. You see the warm yellowy glow of the candles on the walls. You see before you the familiar spiral staircase and you begin to climb each stair. With each step you take upwards, you begin to wake from your comfortable position. 10, you begin to move your fingers and toes, 9, 8, 7, waking fully refreshed, 5, 4, waking fully refreshed and beginning to stretch, 3, fully awake, 2 eyes open, and 1, fully alert and refreshed.

How to dowse to find ghosts and lost objects

For this you will need a pendulum, which (for instance) can be a semi-precious stone on a gold chain or a wedding ring on a piece of string. A pendulum is the easiest and often quickest way of making instant decisions, and this is achieved through accessing the intuitive powers we all possess. It can be used to locate lost objects, find the most healing foods for us, locate nutritional deficiencies within ourselves, and offer guidance in relationship decisions.

Throughout history, people have used dowsing with a pendulum to guide them through their lives and help them make decisions. When circumstances arose during the Vietnam War, for instance, some US marines were taught how to use a pendulum to find tunnels and underground mines.

For hundreds of years, dowsing has been relied on for its accurate ability to find water, gold, and other minerals.

How does it work?

There is no doubt that our inner senses play a part in how the pendulum works. The pendulum is regarded as an antenna, picking up information between the unconscious and the conscious mind, as it is able to detect cues that the conscious mind may not. We have all felt that heavy feeling of dread in the pit of our stomach when entering a building that has perhaps seen tragedy or sadness, or gone to a peaceful location and 'sensed' a feeling of unrest. It is said that the pendulum picks up on this sixth sense.

This is the same sixth sense that animals pick up at the first signs of an approaching thunderstorm, or when a stranger knocks at our front door. We must also consider our higher minds, as the realms of spirit and angelic forces can guide the pendulum. Divination comes from the word divus, which translates to 'our higher self' or 'the God within all of us'.

How do we choose which pendulum to use?

A pendulum is usually a weighted symmetrical object suspended from a single chain or cord, but I have dowsed with pretty much anything, from keys on a fob to a lanyard. The pendulum needs to be weighty enough so it doesn't get blown around when used outside, but not too heavy that it's uncomfortable to use. Weight is down to preference, and personally I prefer a slightly heavier object. My favourite pendulum is a clear quartz stone, shaped into a point and suspended from a chain. I tend to hold the chain halfway down so there's about three inches (7cm) between my fingers and the stone. Most people have their chain around 9cm long, but this is entirely your choice. It is wise to experiment until you are confident you've found the right length for you.

Holding the Pendulum

The pendulum's string, cord, or chain is held between the thumb and forefinger in your dominant hand (the one you write with), although there is another school of thought that suggests it is better to dowse with your non-dominant hand (often the left side) as this is closely related to the right side of the brain (intuition).

What can we use dowsing for?

We can use our pendulum to help us make decisions in topics such as love, business, general well-being, and prosperity. We can also use our pendulums to tap into Earth energies such as ley lines, and for use in Feng Shui to 'rearrange' our homes or places of work.

Dowsing can be used to find the root cause of an illness or dis-ease in the body by passing the pendulum over the body to find the area out of balance and in need of healing.

Pendulums can also tune into ghosts and other entities; it can often detect where spirits appear and can therefore be used in ghost hunting.

We can also use the pendulum to locate lost objects – which can include keys and purses, and any other items belonging to family members who have an emotional connection with that object – with, of course, the need to find it often being the very thing that leads the pendulum to find them. We can also locate missing pets.

Charging your Pendulum

As with any kind of divination, it is important to 'charge' the pendulum, and we can do this by placing crystals around the pendulum in a circle. Amethyst, Rose Quartz, and Clear Quartz are all good semi-precious stones for this purpose. We can hold the pendulum under running water or mineral water whilst at the same time sprinkling salt onto it. We can also dry off the pendulum by placing it outside for a day to absorb the energies from the sun (it doesn't have to be shining) and, of course, the air.

Another way to charge your pendulum is to hold it carefully and safely over the flame from a white candle and say:

'Using the power of this flame, may this pendulum be charged with fire, positivity, and light to guide me in the answers that I seek. May this pendulum give me truthful answers for the highest good of all.'

Then, leave the candle to burn safely.

It is also a good idea to keep your pendulum in a small dark-coloured drawstring bag to keep unwanted energies away and, of course, to protect it from damage.

Finding your pendulum responses

Before you begin, empty your mind of all conscious thoughts. This may require practice. One good way of doing this is to visualise a beautiful clear running stream of water flowing past you in your mind's eye. I sometimes see incoming thoughts as cars going past me. You do not need to try to block thoughts, just let them go by. Pay no attention to them.

When you ask your questions, the responses you get from the pendulum are usually different for everyone, although some directions are more common. A 'Yes' answer, for instance, is usually shown by the pendulum swinging in a clockwise direction, though not necessarily in a perfect circle.

A 'No' response is usually shown by the pendulum swinging in an anti-clockwise direction, although this can be different for some people. It is usually a mirror image of whatever the 'Yes' response is, but not always.

The 'Ask Again' response is usually a back and forth swing indicating that the question is not being phrased correctly or that now is not the right time to be asking the question.

A pendulum that continuously swings in a positive direction can sometimes be a sign that you are on the 'right track'. If you come off track it will swing to the negative response. This is similar to when an excited dog walks a path it is familiar with and pulls on the leash.

Asking the right questions

This is a tricky subject and one that should be thought about carefully, particularly when using your pendulum on behalf of someone else, as it can be difficult to gauge someone else's responses or motives. One must also consider the privacy and free will of other people.

Questions should be phrased as 'Will I', 'Should I', and 'Can I' – you cannot ask for options other than these. Before I begin, I always ask if now is the right time to ask the question, as there could be times when intervention could do more harm than good.

It is also helpful to write down the question, and make sure you do it with a clear intention. Questions like 'Is my health good?' are too vague, and 'Will chocolate make me fat?' is also not useful. Instead we can ask questions like 'Are Brussels sprouts good for my health at the moment?' or 'Is this route the best way to get to work today?' Questions can be many and varied but they have to be clear and concise. Be mindful about requesting the answer to one question whilst thinking of another, as this can give muddled responses.

Questions about timing are also useful and the pendulum will provide clear answers if asked correctly. When standing in a bus queue, for instance, you could ask 'Will the bus I need to catch be on time today?' Or, if it's going to be late you could ask by how many minutes. As you say the numbers in your head, watch as the pendulum swings 'Yes' when you reach the correct number.

Another possibility when it comes to decision-making is to write on a piece of paper the words: 'Yes', 'No', and 'Ask again', spaced out considerably to allow for the swing of the pendulum. This is another way to receive answers to questions, providing your questions are honest and clear.

If we're asking questions in relation to months or even years, we can say each month out loud (not forgetting to say the year as well, as the pendulum needs clarification). This has proven to be very useful to me when I've asked questions, and even the most surprising of answers have been accurate.

Remember to cleanse and charge your pendulum after each use.

This can be done by wafting it through incense smoke, such as white sage or a similar refreshing and cleansing fragrance. Also, washing it in running water and using sprinkled salt is very cleansing.

As with any kind of psychic and divination work, it is always a good idea to place yourself in a bubble of white light beforehand, to breathe slowly and deeply, and to imagine yourself protected and shielded from any unwanted negative energies. You could also light a candle and watch as the candlelight offers a protective light to both you and the pendulum whilst saying 'I call to me my protective guardian (Archangel Michael, or whomever you feel you need to ask) to keep me safe from harm'.

Dowsing with rods can be used when doing fieldwork. If we are out walking and want to find a lost track or landscape feature, such as a river or pond, we can use rods for this. In my opinion, the best types are those that have a covered handle so your hands aren't touching the actual rods. This adds weight to the fact that our hands aren't moving the rods themselves.

Next we can ask the rods to find our own personal directions for each answer. For me, opening out means 'Yes' while the rods crossing means 'No' (see photo). There will often be no movement if you've not phrased the question properly or if it's the wrong time to answer. If you walk forward slowly whilst keeping the question in your mind, you will find that the rods move to give you your answer. Test this first before you set out by placing a glass of water on the ground and asking the rods to show you when they are over the glass of water. Practice builds confidence.

A great way to make decisions when there are many factors involved is to list all your questions and make a note of the response to each question. Your pendulum will insist on honesty and you may find that if you're not being entirely honest with yourself, the pendulum will make this known to you, whether you're conscious of doing so or not.

CONCLUSION

I hope you have enjoyed the stories and accounts in this book, and that you find the resources section useful.

We all have psychic abilities – they're not just for the 'chosen few' – and working with your psychic abilities via daily practice will strengthen the connection you have to both your inner wisdom and your Spirit Guides.

Once you do this, you might find that doors you felt were previously closed to you begin to open – it's all part of our spiritual development, and should you choose to do so, it can assist each and every one of us with evolving and expanding spiritually.

Personally, I intend to continue exploring haunted locations, as well as hopefully discovering the answers to life's big questions.

I am not 100% convinced that our forests in the UK are home to huge hairy bipedal creatures or long-forgotten 'wild men'; I am more inclined to believe that these creatures are interdimensional, travelling across space and time.

Originally, interdimensional travel was thought up by ufologists to explain faster than light appearances by UFOs and other associated phenomena. However, I believe it's also a possible explanation for the appearances and the 'there one minute, gone the next' accounts that many people have told me. This, I believe, is done via the use of portals and magical places that scatter the green pastures of the UK.

My other reasoning for this belief is due to the strange occurrences that appear to go hand in hand with these sightings, such as the silence I mentioned in an earlier chapter and the unusual 'mind probing' that was also reported by the witness at the same time. Headaches, nausea, and feeling 'outside' of oneself are also experienced by many of these witnesses.

Some documentaries describe Bigfoot as an alien, because many of these encounters have been associated with UFO sightings and strange lights in the sky in America. Mind probing and aliens are more common, albeit in other parts of the world; I am not saying this phenomenon doesn't happen in the UK, but it does seem to be more common in the States.

Obviously, I cannot be sure of this but I do know that here in the UK, we are blessed with a large number of wondrous places such as the mystical Avebury Stone Circles, Silbury Hill, and of course Stonehenge – to name but a few.

If you have any stories of your own concerning the strange and mysterious, please contact me as I'd love to hear them. You can do so (and find out more about me) by visiting www. alisoncrocker.co.uk. I look forward to hearing from you.

www.ingramcontent.com/pod-product-compliance
Lightning Source LLC
Chambersburg PA
CBHW050823090426
42738CB00020B/3466